State Shapes

State Shapes Arizona

Text copyright © 2007 by Black Dog & Leventhal Publishers, Inc.

Illustrations copyright © 2007 by Alfred Schrier

Published by
Black Dog & Leventhal Publishers, Inc.
151 W. 19th Street
New York, NY 10011

Distributed by
Workman Publishing Company
225 Varick Street
New York, NY 10014

Manufactured in China

Cover and interior design by Sheila Hart

ISBN-10: 1-57912-701-0

ISBN-13: 978-1-57912-701-5

h g f e d c b a

Library of Congress Cataloging-in-Publication Data is on file at Black Dog & Leventhal Publishers, Inc.

ARIZONA

BY

ERIN MCHUGH

Illustrations by Alfred Schrier

BLACK DOG
& LEVENTHAL
PUBLISHERS
NEW YORK

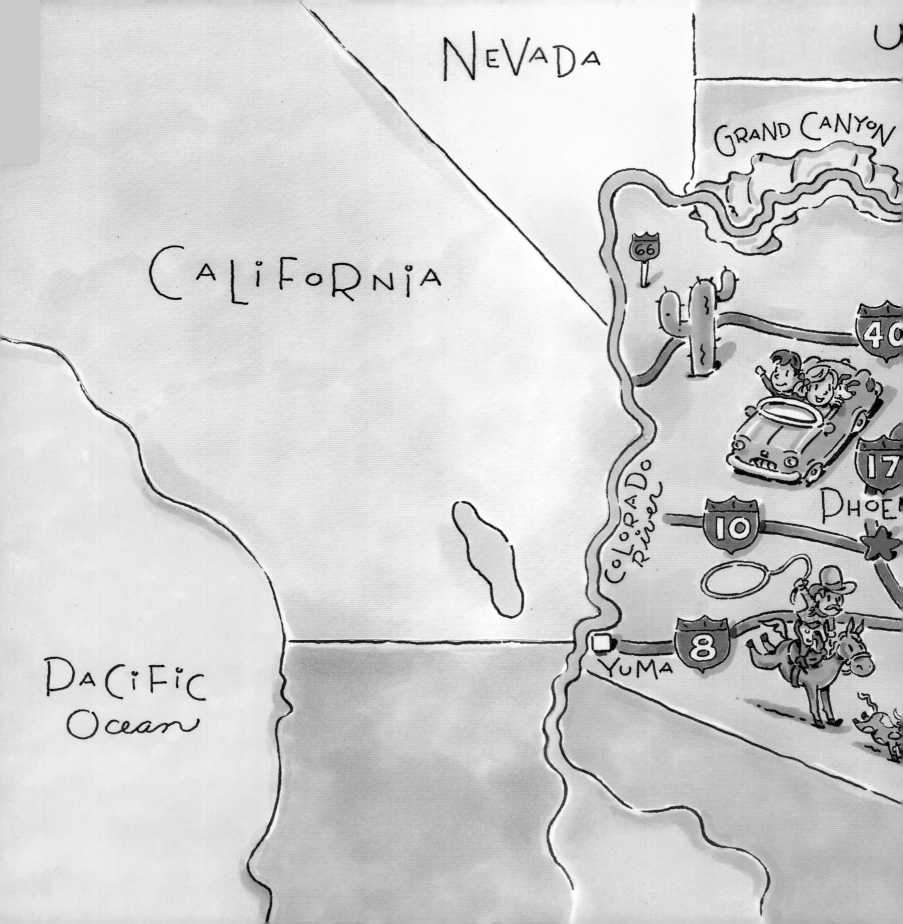

COLORADO

NEW
MEXICO

TEXAS

MEXICO

PAINTED
desert

AGSTAFF
SEDONA

Gold!

MT.
Lemon

SKI

CSON

10

19

Hi there! I'm Leo Francis, your tour guide to the great state of Arizona. In fact, Arizona's better than great—it's *grand*, as in its nickname, "The Grand Canyon State."

It's great—I mean **grand**—to meet you, Leo. My name's Carri, and this is my dog, Scooter. We're totally psyched—we've just moved here!

Well, I think you'll find Arizona pretty cool, Carri. I'm going to take you to see a ghost town, a copper mine, the desert, a rodeo, and lots more.

Sounds awesome!
Whew, it sure is hot. Is the whole state as hot as this?

Nope. Though lots of folks like Arizona *because* it is hot, but it's also nice and dry. A lot of Arizona is in the desert, which is why almost every place is air-conditioned, and lots of streets have misting systems that spray you just a little, to keep you cool while you're outside. But there's great skiing in Arizona too, and the temperature has ranged from 40 degrees below zero once at Hawley Lake to one particularly hot year in Phoenix, when there were 143 days above 100°F!

Q. **What was the hottest temperature ever recorded in Arizona?**

Sounds like it's got everything. How long has your family been here, Leo?

My great-grandmother was a Navajo Indian, so part of my family has been in the area for thousands of years. Native Americans have been here since about 25,000 B.C. Today about 6 million people live in Arizona; 150 years ago, it only had six thousand people! And if you think it's full of retired people playing golf, it's not like that anymore; Arizona has become one of our fastest growing states, full of young families with kids like us. In fact, the average age of residents is thirty-four, which is almost a year younger than the national average.

A. In Lake Havasu City, the mercury climbed to 128°F on June 29, 1994.

We can't wait to see it all. Where do we start?

Right here in Phoenix; it's the capital of Arizona and located smack in the middle of the state. Arizona is an Indian name that means "Place of the Little Spring." In the 1860s, men irrigated the land by digging canals from a nearby river so that they could bring water to the city they were building, which was fertile but dry. So they called the city Phoenix, naming it after the mythical bird that rose out of the ashes. Some folks thought not much would come of it: in 1874, President Ulysses S. Grant said Phoenix was worth just $550. Little did he know! Today it has more people than any other capital city in the United States.

Q. What famous food is Arizona known for?

One of the great things to see in Phoenix is the Desert Botanical Garden. Talk about different, this place is totally amazing! It is filled with 139 different plants that are rare and even endangered, and they've been brought here from every place you can think of.

What's this place with all the bells?

It's called Arcosanti, and it's an experimental town founded by a man named Paolo Soleri. The town is designed according to what Soleri calls "arcology"—part architecture and part ecology. The lights, heating, and cooling in town are all operated with solar power. And those pretty bells you hear are made by volunteers and students; they started selling them to make money for Arcosanti, and now they're sold all over the world.

A. Tortillas and salsa is popular, but some call chile con queso the state food. It's a cheddar cheese dip with bell peppers, tomatoes, chili powder, and chopped onions, and boy is it yummy!

When did settlers start coming to Arizona?

Well, the Mexicans realized there was land north of them that could be rich and fertile; in fact, there had long been a legend that there were "Seven Cities of Cibola." They were supposedly founded by seven bishops from Spain to hide their gold, gems, and religious articles. A Franciscan friar named Marcos de Niza was sent to search for the cities in 1539 and returned saying he had found them in what we now call New Mexico. But many historians believe he never actually went that far—some even call him "the lying monk." Nevertheless, the legend started lots of exploration by the Spanish here in this part of the United States.

Q. Where can you be in four different U.S. states at the same time?

So how did Arizona become part of the United States?

It was bought—in a deal called the Gadsden Purchase. In 1848, after the Mexican-American War, there was still a disagreement about where the border between the two countries was. Some American investors wanted to build a railroad, so one of them, James Gadsden, was sent to negotiate where the border would be. This land of

Arizona became the final boundaries of the continental United States. Around this time, traders and trappers were beginning to settle here, and lots of prospectors came looking for gold, still believing the old fable of Marcos de Niza. Of course the Seven Cities were never found, and though there is some gold here in Arizona, people mostly moved on to the Gold Rush in California.

 A. At the Four Corners, the only place in the United States where four states meet in one place. You can put your hands and feet in Arizona, Utah, Colorado, and New Mexico!

So Phoenix is a city...but in the desert?

Yup. It's called the Sonoran Desert, and it covers 120,000 square miles. The entire state of Rhode Island is only 1,545 square miles, so this is one gigantic desert! It's got lots of plants and animals you might think are really exotic. Then there are gila monsters—which are really lizards— bobcats, scorpions, black widow spiders, and lots of snakes, like the diamondback rattlesnake and the coral snake.

Yikes! It sounds scary roaming around so close to so many snakes.

It's not really that scary; sometimes you just have to watch where you step. After all, they were here first! Besides, there's also the coyote and the roadrunner, just like in the cartoons. The roadrunner weighs less than a pound and can run almost twenty miles per hour. He steers with his tail.

Q. What Arizona sports teams are named after desert animals?

Didn't the famous architect, Frank Lloyd Wright, live out here in the desert?

That's right, Carri. He built a place he called Taliesin West, in Scottsdale. He designed it as both his home and a school to teach young architects "organic architecture." Wright thought that buildings should be part of the landscape and that local materials— like wood and stone from the area—should be used whenever possible. Even though Frank Lloyd Wright died many years ago, students from all over the world still consider it a great honor to come here and learn.

A. The Cardinals and Rattlers, which are both football teams, the Coyotes, which is a hockey team, and the baseball World Series-winning Diamondbacks.

What's that up ahead? That **definitely** does not belong here. It looks like pictures I've seen of old England!

You must mean London Bridge. At one time it really was falling down, just like the nursery rhyme says. When they decided to build a new bridge in London back in the 1960s, they put the old one up for sale and someone bought it and moved it here to Lake Havasu. Now there is an English-looking village built all around it, with double-decker buses driving around town and everything!

And speaking of water, are those houseboats, Leo?

You bet. People rent them for vacationing on Lake Mead, which was one of the four man-made lakes formed when the Hoover Dam was built on the state line between Arizona and Nevada in the 1930s.

Q. What is El Camino del Diablo?

Lake Mead is the biggest reservoir in the United States and not only supplies much needed water throughout the West by controlling the flow of the Colorado River, but is the source of much of the electric power in Arizona. You can motor around Lake Mead on your houseboat for a long time—there's 550 miles of shoreline.

Isn't there another famous man-made lake in Arizona?

Yup, Lake Powell, up north on the Utah border, is also a reservoir, and some say it's the most beautiful lake in the whole country. At 186 miles long, it took fourteen years just to fill it up once it was built! Can you believe that?

 A. Translated it means "The Devil's Highway"; it was once the road that lots of people traveled from Mexico to California in an attempt to join the Gold Rush.

So is this the same Colorado River at the top of the Hoover Dam that's waaaaaay down at the bottom of this big canyon?

Yes, it is, Carri, and here we are at last: the Grand Canyon. Careful! You almost don't see the Grand Canyon until you're right on top of it. It's more than a mile deep, and in some places it's more than eighteen miles wide. It's one of the Seven Wonders of the Natural World. Over the course of millions of years, the Colorado River, along with ice and wind, has helped carve out the Grand Canyon. Some scientists even think it was once an ocean, but no one can really be sure.

Q. Why were camels brought to Arizona in the 1850s?

It was an explorer and Civil War hero named Major John Wesley Powell who first called it the "Grand Canyon." In 1869, he led nine other adventurous explorers on a trip of over 1,000 miles down the Colorado River and through the Grand Canyon.

He sounds awfully brave.

You can't even imagine! Major Powell did all this exploration with just one arm; he had lost his other arm fighting in the Civil War. And they had to ride the rapids in these flimsy boats, not exactly like the whitewater rafting people do for fun on vacations these days.

A. Jefferson Davis, then secretary of war, brought camels over from Turkey when men were building roads across the desert out west. The camels were used for a short time to carry freight and communications.

17

Can people go down to the bottom of the Canyon?

Oh sure, there are lots of ways to see the Grand Canyon besides just walking the rim, as the edge is called. People go rafting down the Colorado River with expert guides nowadays; it's safe and lots of people like to try it. But you can also hike all the way to the bottom, go off-road in a Hummer, or even fly on a plane or helicopter sightseeing tour. But that's not my favorite way to go. I'll show you.

You're crazy, Leo—no way!

Hop on, guys. Ride 'em! We're going to see the bottom of the Grand Canyon, just like I promised—on a mule! It's a long ride down Bright Angel Trail; it'll take five and a half hours, even though it's just ten miles long. In a car on the highway,

Q. Why does a cactus have needles?

18

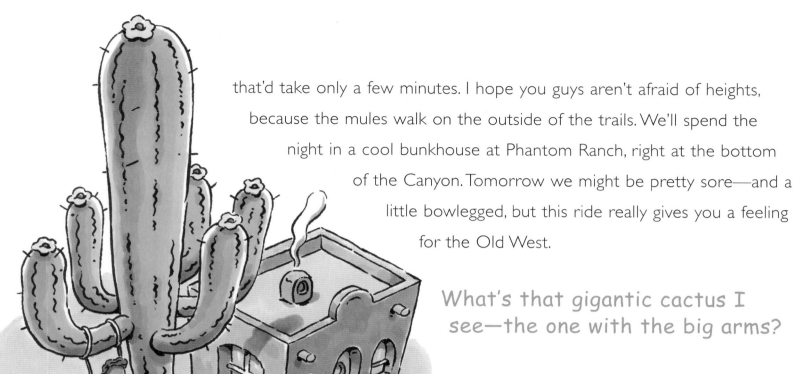

that'd take only a few minutes. I hope you guys aren't afraid of heights, because the mules walk on the outside of the trails. We'll spend the night in a cool bunkhouse at Phantom Ranch, right at the bottom of the Canyon. Tomorrow we might be pretty sore—and a little bowlegged, but this ride really gives you a feeling for the Old West.

What's that gigantic cactus I see—the one with the big arms?

It's called a saguaro, and the tallest one in Arizona is fifty-seven feet, eleven inches, which is taller than most houses! Their "arms" don't even begin to grow until they're about sixty-five years old, and they can live one hundred years after that. The saguaro flower is Arizona's state flower; it blooms at night, only once, and never blooms again. Some birds poke holes in saguaros and make themselves a nesting place.

 The needles, or spines, keep animals from drinking the water inside the cactus that keeps the plant alive.

From this map, it looks like a lot of Arizona is an Indian reservation.

Yep. Almost all of the northeastern part of the state is the Navajo Indian Reservation, or Navajo Nation. It covers 27,000 square miles and also goes into parts of Utah and New Mexico. It's the largest area of land set aside for Native Americans in the country. The Apaches are closely related to the Navajos and live there too, and there's also a smaller Hopi reservation. I see some teepees over there; there must a tribal meeting going on. Most American Indians live in houses now.

Many of the people make their living doing the things Native Americans did so long ago. They herd sheep and cattle, weave, and make beautiful jewelry and art. You'll see them selling their wares at stands on the side of the road. You can take home some pottery!

(map labels: Kaibab, Hualapi, ARIZONA, Gila, Navajo & Apache, fort Apache, Papago)

Q. How is a teepee different from a wigwam?

I've heard about Geronimo and Cochise. Were they Navajos?

Actually, they were both Apaches. They lived about two hundred years ago and were great warriors; Geronimo was a medicine man and considered a seer, which is someone who can predict the future. Unfortunately, there was much fighting and many, many Native Americans died at the hands of the white man, including the families of both Geronimo and Cochise. Today our government and Native American leaders are still meeting to try and make up for some of the terrible things that occurred in the past. After all, the people of the Navajo Nation were here long before the white man was.

 A. A teepee is a cone-shaped structure of stripped tree saplings covered with cloth. A wigwam is dome shaped and often covered with natural things like grass, brush, bark, and reeds.

I think I'm going to love it here in Arizona. It's so different than anywhere I've ever been.

Well, there's still a lot of the Old West here, and I think it's fun to be reminded of some of Arizona's vibrant history. For example, did you know Arizona still has a Pony Express, which was an early way of delivering mail by horseback? Well, once a year, anyway. Riders dressed as cowboys do a two hundred-mile relay over three days carrying over 20,000 pieces of mail, passing it off to each other along the route, racing to get to their destination as fast as they can. People cheer them on and eat and drink with them at saloons along the way; you can even send a letter to someone that says "via Pony Express," and that's the way it'll be delivered.

Too bad Scooter's not big enough to ride on!

Q. What is Arizonan Charles Mingus known for?

And just to be even more different, Arizona is the only state in the continental United States that doesn't observe daylight savings time. They do observe it in the Navajo Nation, but everywhere else, no one wanted to deal with daylight savings time. Part of the reason for daylight savings is to give the farmers another hour of light for work. But it's so warm here, people don't want another hour of hot sun!

 He was one of the greatest bass players who ever lived. Born in Phoenix, he played a major part in the growth of jazz as an art form in the twentieth century and founded a musical think tank called the Jazz Workshop.

Wait a second! What the heck are those?!

Bet you think those tracks are so big they could belong to a dinosaur. Well, you're right! We've just arrived in the Petrified Forest National Park, and scientists have recently discovered the footprints and fossils of the coelophysis here; it's one of the oldest dinosaurs known, from the late Triassic period. You'll also see tons of petrified wood, which are fossils; it's fossil wood, and its original materials have been replaced by minerals over millions of years.

That's unbelievable.

Q. Which Supreme Court Justice was raised in Arizona?

I'll bet that's the Painted Desert up ahead.

You can't miss the Painted Desert; it looks like a layer cake. In the sunset, the mountains turn red, pink, orange, and purple. It's the minerals and eons of decaying organic matter that make them look that way. You might recognize that red clay color; the Navajos use it to make some of the pottery we saw at their roadside stands.

Is that a giant pueblo over there?

It's the Painted Desert Inn. Everyone called it "the Stone Tree House" when it was built. (Not like stone *tree house*, but *stone tree* house, because of the petrified wood.) When it was built in 1924, it was a real oasis for travelers. There weren't many good highways, and cars weren't very dependable, so folks stopped here for food and drinks and beautiful views of the Painted Desert. It was so rustic that water had to be carted in from ten miles away.

 Sandra Day O'Connor grew up on a cattle ranch in Duncan. She was the first female Supreme Court Justice in history.

What were the roads like back then?

Well, the most famous road ever in America was Route 66, which was called "the Mother Road." It pretty much disappeared once the big highways and interstates were built in the second half of the twentieth century. Route 66 went from Chicago, Illinois, all the way to Santa Monica, California—that's 2,248 miles and three time zones! The longest stretch of it was in Arizona, but it also traveled through Illinois, Missouri, Kansas, Oklahoma, Texas, New Mexico, and California.

They started paving Route 66 in 1926: it went right through the Petrified Forest at Winslow, so business was good at the Painted Desert Inn. Then it went on through Williams, which is the gateway to the Grand Canyon, and Flagstaff, the highest point on all of Route 66, and it passed through Topock before it continued on into California.

Q. Who were the Navajo "code talkers?"

Hey, here we are coming into Flagstaff now.
You know, that's a funny name for a town.

I know, but there's a good reason for it. In 1876, some people from Boston asked that one of these beautiful, tall Ponderosa pine trees be made into a giant flag pole to celebrate our country's centennial, which was a celebration across the nation when America was one hundred years old.

Flagstaff is one of the highest cities in the country—you can even go skiing nearby. But maybe the coolest thing is the Lowell Observatory, right here in Flagstaff. Astronomers discovered "dwarf planet" Pluto through this humongous telescope in 1930.

 A. In World War II, the government hired Navajos to translate and communicate secret military messages. Since the Navajo language is unwritten, with no alphabet or symbols, the enemy was completely baffled, and this helped us win the war.

Leo, check out that gigantic hole!

That's no hole, but you may not even believe me when I tell you what it is: it's a meteor crater! In fact, the name of this town is Meteor Crater, Arizona. Sometimes it's called the Barringer Meteorite Crater after the mining engineer who spent years researching the mystery of how this hole appeared in the middle of the desert. Scientists eventually agreed that it was most likely a meteorite originating from the inside of a small planet that had fallen to earth about 50,000 years ago, speeding towards us at a rate of 28,600 miles per hour. The hole is nearly a mile wide and 570 feet deep.

Q. What is Arizona's official amphibian?

I keep thinking I'm going to see some cowboys ride by.

Funny you should say that, because this is where writer Zane Grey got the inspiration for his western novels. Early in the twentieth century Zane came here with a friend to hunt mountain lions; he fell in love with Arizona and began to write about it. Some say one of his characters was the basis for the old Lone Ranger westerns from the early days of television. Zane's books were so popular that he became one of the first authors to make more than a million dollars, and that was a bundle in his day too!

RIBBIT.

 It's the Arizona tree frog, a tiny thing that measures only about two inches long at its biggest. They live in oak, pine, and fir trees, gobbling up insects.

I sure have seen a lot of cows on this trip.

Actually, that's cattle you've seen. The three industries Arizonans make the most money from are raising cattle, growing cotton, and mining copper. These industries make up a large part of Arizona's economy. There are about 800,000 heads of cattle in the state, but that's not all. Farmers and ranchers also raise about 115,000 hogs, 140,000 sheep, 38,000 goats, 350,000 chickens, 18,500 emus and ostriches, and 55,000 colonies of bees! That means they also produce almost 3 billion pounds of milk, 81 million eggs, and over 3 million pounds of honey!

Q. Where is there a buried treasure in Arizona?

Wow, people here sure know how to live off the land. But speaking of farming, didn't Cesar Chavez grow up in Arizona?

He sure did; he was born and raised near Yuma, in the western part of the state. Cesar only went to school through the eighth grade because he had to help support his family. He worked as a migrant laborer himself and he eventually founded the union that became the United Farm Workers. He spent his life organizing laborers and fighting for them to get better wages and rights. He received the Presidential Medal of Freedom, and in some states, his birthday is even a holiday.

 A. No one knows for sure, but legend has it that "Bronco Bill" Walters hid money from some Wells Fargo stagecoach robberies near Solomonville—and it hasn't been seen since!

**And what about all this corn?
And those fields over there?**

Corn is a huge crop for Arizonans. Not only does it feed much of the nation, but it feeds the cattle, chicken, and other animals here too.

**Hey, where are those kids going?
It looks like fun!**

That's a corn maze, and they're awesome. Do you get the joke? *Maize* was the word the Indians used for corn back in the Pilgrim days. But this corn maze is something the farmers construct right in the cornfields. They make paths by cutting down cornstalks in the fields, and you try to see if you can figure out the route and come out the other end.

Q. What is a bolo tie?

If you fly over in a plane, you'll see some of the farmers have cut the corn so it makes pictures—cowboys, sports team logos, American flags—all kinds of neat stuff.

I can see how a cowboy could get mighty lonesome out here in the fields.

Well, there's been a long tradition of writing what's called cowboy poetry, and nowadays there are contests and events and even a Cowboy Poetry Week. It's very popular here in Arizona. As you can imagine, cowboys had lots of free time and often wrote songs or poems because they were easy to memorize and pass on by singing or recitation. Carrying a lot of books around on horseback was not practical on the range, so writing everything down was often out of the question.

A. It's the official Arizona neckwear and was invented in the 1940s by silversmith Victor Cedarstaff when he detached a hatband with a fancy silver buckle from his hat and looped it around his neck for safekeeping.

Say, Leo, what's that up there? It looks like a pueblo apartment building.

It's called Montezuma's Castle; they're cliff dwellings, and over six hundred years ago the Sinagua Indians lived there. Montezuma's Well is nearby too, and it was where the Sinaguas got their water. Mysteries surround both places, though—neither geologists nor archaeologists can figure out the source of the water, and the tribe that lived in the cliffs just seems to have disappeared around the 1400s. Still, how cool must it have been to live in those rocks, high above everything?

Q. What is the Cactus League?

You're right, what about those crazy rocks up ahead—one looks just like Snoopy!

They're called the Red Rocks, and you can see why. There definitely was an ocean here once—maybe 300 million years ago—and when the water receded, it left these wild shapes: arches, spires, even Snoopy! Other famous spots are Bell Rock and Cathedral Rock. They're red because they're made of sandstone, which contains iron oxide. You know how if you leave something made of metal out in the rain it gets rusty? That's pretty much what happened here—there's rust in them thar hills!

Let's go over to Slide Rock—it's a natural waterslide, and we can go for a few wild rides. Yaaahoo!

 Baseball's spring training! Lots of Major League Baseball teams practice for their regular season by playing each other in Mesa, Arizona, every year in late winter and early spring.

This looks sort of like a hippie town. And what's that music?

We're in Sedona. Besides being a really pretty town, it's become a place to live and visit for people who are interested in New Age philosophy.

What's that?

New Age people think we should be open-minded and that everything we do should be done with both our minds and hearts. They say the mind has powers we don't even know about and that certain things we find in the earth, such as crystals, help open our minds and hearts. And then there are the world-famous Sedona vortexes.

Q. What do kids all over the world have Joan Ganz Cooney to thank for?

Vortexes?

A vortex is a very unusual type of magnetic energy in the earth; they're very rare, and Sedona has *four* of them. People swear they can feel the energy of the vortexes and that it helps clear the mind and brings a kind of peace. It's all sort of heavenly sounding, isn't it?

I don't know...

I promise you'll find wonderful people here—artists, psychics, healers, and others who believe that Sedona is the spiritual center of the earth.

A. Sesame Street! The Phoenix-native created the long-running program in 1969.

Arizona has so much stuff to see, Leo. My head is spinning.

You'll really like this stop, Carri, though you might find it a little spooky. Welcome to Jerome! There are 275 ghost towns in Arizona alone, but Jerome is the biggest one in the whole country. Ghost towns were once old mining towns; Jerome was near a copper mine, which as you remember, is a big part of Arizona's economy. Since the 1800s, people would flock to live in places where a new mine was about to open. There would be plenty of jobs, and these towns would spring up almost overnight. But when they dug up everything they could and the mines were empty, everybody just moved someplace else and these old towns were left vacant. Believe it or not,

Q. Arizona's weather has long prompted people to move here and retire. What business, catering to retirees, started here?

this quiet little town was once known as "the Wickedest Town in the West" because there were so many saloons. Back when the mine was really busy about a hundred years ago, they would mine 3 million pounds of copper in a month.

It's funny. The town **does** have a spooky feeling, but it looks like there are some real live people here too, in some of these old buildings.

That's right. Back in the 1960s and '70s, all kinds of artists, musicians, writers, and craftsmen moved here. "Ghost City" was just an empty town waiting for them. Oh, and by the way, they say there really *are* ghosts here. Even the old inn is supposed to be haunted!

A. The very first old age home in America opened for pioneers in Prescott, Arizona in 1911.

I heard there used to be a TV show about Arizona during the Old West days.

You're right, Carri. It was called "Tombstone Territory." There was another show too called "Wyatt Earp," and he was a real sheriff. He and his brothers are all part of the Tombstone legend; around here it's called the "Old West" now, but back then it was really the "*Wild* West." Life was pretty lawless out here, and some say the lawmen were the baddest bunch of all. Back in October of 1881, the Earp brothers and their friend "Doc" Holliday got into a shootout with some cowboys whom they accused of being horse and cattle thieves.

I've heard about that!
It was called "the Gunfight at the OK Corral."

Q. Whatever happened to Wyatt Earp?

Yup. And one of the reasons it's so famous is that folks are still fighting about whose fault it was. You might just assume that Wyatt Earp and his friends were in the right because they were the "good guys." But they had a grudge with a couple of these cowpokes, and to this day no one is really sure if they had the right to shoot the so-called thieves. But it's an example of how rough-and-tumble things were back then in Tombstone.

Whoa! But how did Tombstone get its name?

Well, at one time there was lots of gold and silver in these parts. But it was so dangerous to live here that everyone said you'd probably find your tombstone before you were lucky enough to find any gold or silver!

 He went to jail twice for stealing and finally opened a saloon in San Diego, California.

What's that big parade up ahead, Leo?

You'll never see another parade like this, Carri. This is Tucson, and every year the rodeo season for the whole country pretty much starts here at La Fiesta de los Vaqueros—that means Celebration of the Cowboys. Because it's a parade for the rodeo, nothing with a motor is allowed. Tons of people come to see it, and kids even get two days off from school.

Yee-ha! And everybody in town is wearing Western outfits!

That's right! There's roping and riding, and all the biggest rodeo cowboys are here. An interesting thing about the rodeo is that it began as an offshoot of an industry: cowboys were already rustling and roping animals every day, and they started to make a contest out of it.

Q. How much copper is on the roof of Arizona's capitol building in Phoenix?

It looks like people have painted on the walls of buildings all over town! Won't they get in trouble?

Trouble? Not at all! In fact, sometimes local businesses and government even help pay for the artists to paint them. It's called Chicano mural painting, and it's been a big art movement here in Tucson since the 1970s. Chicano is slang for Mexican-American, and since we're near the Mexican border, many of the murals are about Chicano culture. Sometimes the artists let the neighborhood kids help.

Maybe they'll let us paint!

A. The amount of copper is equal to 4,800,000 pennies—or $48,000.

How about that mining tour you promised us, Leo?

Sure, we're at the Copper Queen Mine, here in Bisbee. This was a humongous mine that was open for almost one hundred years, closing in 1974. Almost 3 billion pounds of copper came out of this mine. Because it's an old mining camp, some folks call Bisbee a ghost town, but the citizens here are very sensitive about that. They say the town and its economy are as lively as ever. With the tours, even the old Copper Queen is still making money!

Wow, our trip is almost over, Leo; I would love to buy some souvenirs.

Q. What was the largest bank robbery ever in U.S. history?

Then don't forget about Arizona's beautiful state gem—turquoise. In the old days, Native Americans thought turquoise had magical powers, and they would wear it for good luck; they thought it kept away illness too. However, if you lost some turquoise, it was said you would get so sick you would have to see the medicine man. The Navajo Indians have long been making silver and turquoise jewelry. But turquoise has also been found on mummies in Egypt from as far back as 5,000 B.C. Even today, it's probably the most popular thing tourists take home from Arizona.

It's gorgeous! I want a belt for me, a collar for Scooter, and gifts for everyone in my family. Leo, Arizona is such a fascinating state. We're going to love living here!

 A. The Weathermen, a radical political student group from the 1960s, robbed a bank in Tucson of $33 million.

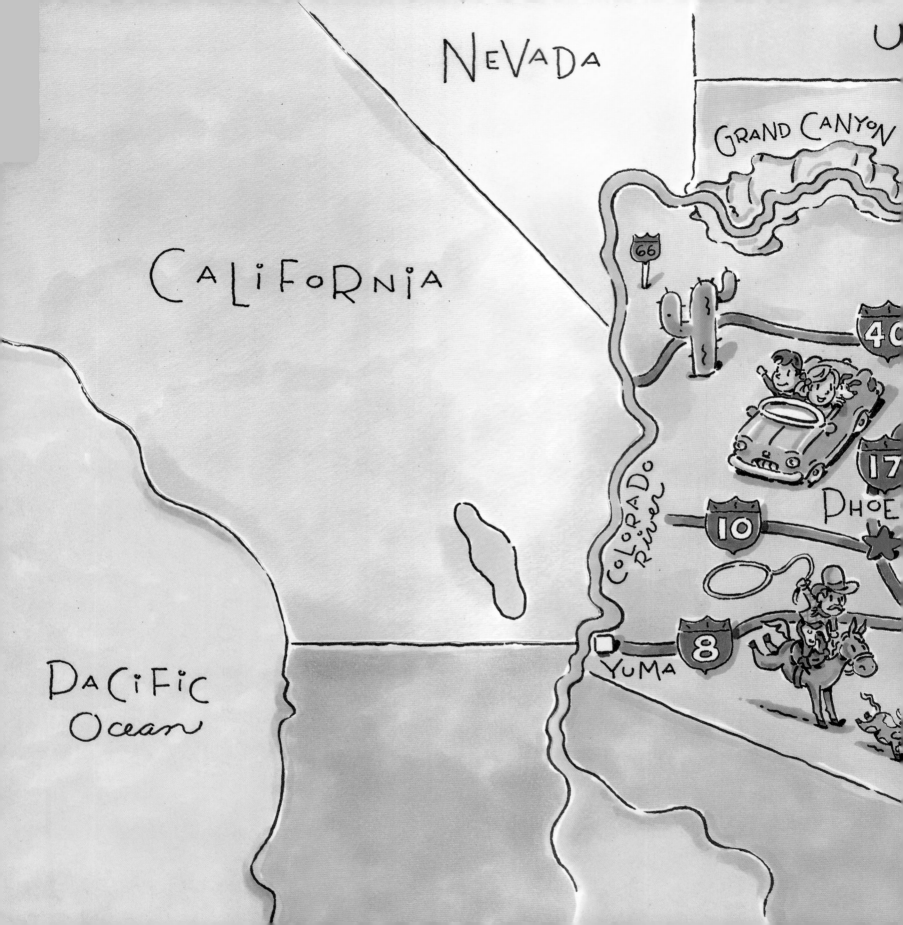

H

COLORADO

PAINTED
desert

AGSTAFF
SEDONA

Gold!

MT.
Lemon

SKI

CSON

10

19

NEW
MEXICO

TEXAS

MEXICO

STATE SHAPES